CORNELL
Notebook

This book belongs to:

_____

_____

_____

I hope you enjoyed this book.

I am a small independent publisher and I love creating books just like this and it would mean the world to me if you could spend just a minute to share your experience on Amazon. It would really help a lot. :-)

SCAN ME

TABLE OF CONTENTS

DATE	TOPIC	PAGE

TABLE OF CONTENTS

DATE	TOPIC	PAGE

TABLE OF CONTENTS

DATE	TOPIC	PAGE

TABLE OF CONTENTS

DATE	TOPIC	PAGE
DATE	TOPIC	PAGE

Class		Date		
Topic		Continued from Page:		

Main Points	Notes

	Continued on page:	

Summary:

1

Class		Date	
Topic		Continued from Page:	

Main Points	Notes

Continued on page:

Summary:

Class		Date	
Topic		Continued from Page:	

Main Points	Notes

Continued on page:

Summary:

Class			Date	
Topic			Continued from Page:	

Main Points	Notes

Continued on page:

Summary:

Class		Date	
Topic		Continued from Page:	

Main Points	Notes

Continued on page:

Summary:

Class		Date	
Topic		Continued from Page:	

Main Points	Notes

Continued on page:

Summary:

Class		Date	
Topic		Continued from Page:	

Main Points	Notes

Continued on page:

Summary:

Class		Date	
Topic		Continued from Page:	

Main Points	Notes

Continued on page:

Summary:

Class		Date	
Topic		Continued from Page:	

Main Points	Notes

Continued on page:

Summary:

Class		Date	
Topic		Continued from Page:	

Main Points	Notes

Continued on page:

Summary:

Class		Date	
Topic		Continued from Page:	

Main Points	Notes

Continued on page:

Summary:

Class		Date	
Topic		Continued from Page:	

Main Points	Notes

Continued on page:

Summary:

Class		Date	
Topic		Continued from Page:	

Main Points	Notes

Continued on page:

Summary:

Class			Date	
Topic			Continued from Page:	

Main Points	Notes

Continued on page:

Summary:

Class		Date	
Topic		Continued from Page:	

Main Points	Notes

Continued on page:

Summary:

Class		Date	
Topic		Continued from Page:	

Main Points	Notes

Continued on page:

Summary:

Class		Date	
Topic		Continued from Page:	

Main Points	Notes

Continued on page:

Summary:

Class		Date	
Topic		Continued from Page:	

Main Points	Notes

Continued on page:

Summary:

Class		Date	
Topic		Continued from Page:	

Main Points	Notes

Continued on page:

Summary:

Class		Date	
Topic		Continued from Page:	

Main Points	Notes

Continued on page:

Summary:

Class		Date	
Topic		Continued from Page:	

Main Points	Notes

Continued on page:

Summary:

Class		Date	
Topic		Continued from Page:	

Main Points	Notes

Continued on page:

Summary:

Class		Date	
Topic		Continued from Page:	

Main Points	Notes

Continued on page:

Summary:

Class		Date	
Topic		Continued from Page:	

Main Points	Notes

Continued on page:

Summary:

Class		Date	
Topic		Continued from Page:	

Main Points	Notes

Continued on page:

Summary:

Class		Date	
Topic		Continued from Page:	

Main Points	Notes

Continued on page:

Summary:

Class		Date	
Topic		Continued from Page:	

Main Points	Notes

Continued on page:

Summary:

Class		Date	
Topic		Continued from Page:	

Main Points	Notes

Continued on page:

Summary:

Class		Date	
Topic		Continued from Page:	

Main Points	Notes

Continued on page:

Summary:

Class		Date	
Topic		Continued from Page:	

Main Points	Notes

Continued on page:

Summary:

Class		Date	
Topic		Continued from Page:	

Main Points	Notes

Continued on page:

Summary:

Class			Date	
Topic			Continued from Page:	

Main Points	Notes

Continued on page:

Summary:

Class		Date	
Topic		Continued from Page:	

Main Points	Notes

	Continued on page:	

Summary:

33

Class		Date	
Topic		Continued from Page:	

Main Points	Notes

Continued on page:

Summary:

Class		Date	
Topic		Continued from Page:	

Main Points	Notes

Continued on page:

Summary:

Class		Date	
Topic		Continued from Page:	

Main Points	Notes

Continued on page:

Summary:

Class		Date	
Topic		Continued from Page:	

Main Points	Notes

Continued on page:

Summary:

Class		Date	
Topic		Continued from Page:	

Main Points	Notes

Continued on page:

Summary:

Class		Date	
Topic		Continued from Page:	

Main Points	Notes

Continued on page:

Summary:

Class			Date	
Topic			Continued from Page:	

Main Points	Notes

	Continued on page:

Summary:

Class			Date	
Topic			Continued from Page:	

Main Points	Notes

Continued on page:

Summary:

Class		Date	
Topic		Continued from Page:	

Main Points	Notes

Continued on page:

Summary:

Class		Date	
Topic		Continued from Page:	

Main Points	Notes

Continued on page:

Summary:

Class		Date	
Topic		Continued from Page:	

Main Points	Notes

Continued on page:

Summary:

Class		Date	
Topic		Continued from Page:	

Main Points	Notes

	Continued on page:	

Summary:

45

Class		Date	
Topic		Continued from Page:	

Main Points	Notes

Continued on page:

Summary:

Class		Date	
Topic		Continued from Page:	

Main Points	Notes

Continued on page:

Summary:

Class		Date	
Topic		Continued from Page:	

Main Points	Notes

Continued on page:

Summary:

Class		Date	
Topic		Continued from Page:	

Main Points	Notes

Continued on page:

Summary:

Class		Date	
Topic		Continued from Page:	

Main Points	Notes

Continued on page:

Summary:

Class		Date	
Topic		Continued from Page:	

Main Points	Notes

Continued on page:

Summary:

Class		Date	
Topic		Continued from Page:	

Main Points	Notes

Continued on page:

Summary:

Class		Date	
Topic		Continued from Page:	

Main Points	Notes

Continued on page:

Summary:

Class			Date	
Topic			Continued from Page:	

Main Points	Notes

Continued on page:

Summary:

Class		Date	
Topic		Continued from Page:	

Main Points	Notes

Continued on page:

Summary:

Class		Date	
Topic		Continued from Page:	

Main Points	Notes

Continued on page:

Summary:

Class		Date	
Topic		Continued from Page:	

Main Points	Notes

	Continued on page:	

Summary:

57

Class		Date	
Topic		Continued from Page:	

Main Points	Notes

Continued on page:

Summary:

Class		Date	
Topic		Continued from Page:	

Main Points	Notes

Continued on page:

Summary:

Class			Date	
Topic			Continued from Page:	

Main Points	Notes

Continued on page:

Summary:

Class			Date	
Topic			Continued from Page:	

Main Points	Notes

Continued on page:

Summary:

61

Class		Date	
Topic		Continued from Page:	

Main Points	Notes

Continued on page:

Summary:

Class		Date	
Topic		Continued from Page:	

Main Points	Notes

Continued on page:

Summary:

Class		Date	
Topic		Continued from Page:	

Main Points	Notes

Continued on page:

Summary:

Class		Date	
Topic		Continued from Page:	

Main Points	Notes

Continued on page:

Summary:

65

Class		Date	
Topic		Continued from Page:	

Main Points	Notes

Continued on page:

Summary:

Class		Date	
Topic		Continued from Page:	

Main Points	Notes

Continued on page:

Summary:

Class		Date	
Topic		Continued from Page:	

Main Points	Notes

Continued on page:

Summary:

Class			Date	
Topic			Continued from Page:	

Main Points	Notes

Continued on page:

Summary:

Class		Date	
Topic		Continued from Page:	

Main Points	Notes

		Continued on page:	

Summary:

70

Class		Date	
Topic		Continued from Page:	

Main Points	Notes

Continued on page:

Summary:

Class		Date	
Topic		Continued from Page:	

Main Points	Notes

Continued on page:

Summary:

Class			Date	
Topic			Continued from Page:	

Main Points	Notes
	Continued on page:

Summary:

Class		Date	
Topic		Continued from Page:	

Main Points	Notes

Continued on page:

Summary:

Class		Date	
Topic		Continued from Page:	

Main Points	Notes

Continued on page:

Summary:

Class		Date	
Topic		Continued from Page:	

Main Points	Notes

Continued on page:

Summary:

Class		Date	
Topic		Continued from Page:	

Main Points	Notes

Continued on page:

Summary:

Class			Date	
Topic			Continued from Page:	

Main Points	Notes

Continued on page:

Summary:

Class		Date	
Topic		Continued from Page:	

Main Points	Notes

Continued on page:

Summary:

Class		Date	
Topic		Continued from Page:	

Main Points	Notes

Continued on page:

Summary:

Class		Date	
Topic		Continued from Page:	

Main Points	Notes

Continued on page:

Summary:

Class		Date	
Topic		Continued from Page:	

Main Points	Notes

Continued on page:

Summary:

Class		Date	
Topic		Continued from Page:	

Main Points	Notes

Continued on page:

Summary:

Class		Date	
Topic		Continued from Page:	

Main Points	Notes
	Continued on page:

Summary:

Class		Date	
Topic		Continued from Page:	

Main Points	Notes
	Continued on page:

Summary:

Class		Date	
Topic		Continued from Page:	

Main Points	Notes

Continued on page:

Summary:

Class		Date	
Topic		Continued from Page:	

Main Points	Notes

Continued on page:

Summary:

Class		Date	
Topic		Continued from Page:	

Main Points	Notes
	Continued on page:

Summary:

Class		Date	
Topic		Continued from Page:	

Main Points	Notes

Continued on page:

Summary:

Class		Date	
Topic		Continued from Page:	

Main Points	Notes

Continued on page:

Summary:

Class		Date	
Topic		Continued from Page:	

Main Points	Notes

Continued on page:

Summary:

Class		Date	
Topic		Continued from Page:	

Main Points	Notes

Continued on page:

Summary:

Class		Date	
Topic		Continued from Page:	

Main Points	Notes

Continued on page:

Summary:

Class		Date	
Topic		Continued from Page:	

Main Points	Notes

Continued on page:

Summary:

Class		Date	
Topic		Continued from Page:	

Main Points	Notes

	Continued on page:

Summary:

Class		Date	
Topic		Continued from Page:	

Main Points	Notes

Continued on page:

Summary:

Class		Date	
Topic		Continued from Page:	

Main Points	Notes

	Continued on page:	

Summary:

97

Class		Date	
Topic		Continued from Page:	

Main Points	Notes

Continued on page:

Summary:

Class		Date	
Topic		Continued from Page:	

Main Points	Notes
	Continued on page:

Summary:

Class		Date	
Topic		Continued from Page:	

Main Points	Notes

Continued on page:

Summary:

Class		Date	
Topic		Continued from Page:	

Main Points	Notes

Continued on page:

Summary:

Class		Date	
Topic		Continued from Page:	

Main Points	Notes
	Continued on page:

Summary:

Class		Date	
Topic		Continued from Page:	

Main Points	Notes

Continued on page:

Summary:

Class		Date	
Topic		Continued from Page:	

Main Points	Notes

Continued on page:

Summary:

Class		Date	
Topic		Continued from Page:	

Main Points	Notes

Continued on page:

Summary:

Class		Date	
Topic		Continued from Page:	

Main Points	Notes

Continued on page:

Summary:

Class		Date	
Topic		Continued from Page:	

Main Points	Notes

	Continued on page:	

Summary:

Class		Date	
Topic		Continued from Page:	

Main Points	Notes

Summary:

Class		Date	
Topic		Continued from Page:	

Main Points	Notes

Continued on page:

Summary:

Class		Date	
Topic		Continued from Page:	

Main Points	Notes

Continued on page:

Summary:

Class		Date	
Topic		Continued from Page:	

Main Points	Notes

Continued on page:

Summary:

Class		Date	
Topic		Continued from Page:	

Main Points	Notes

Continued on page:

Summary:

Class		Date	
Topic		Continued from Page:	

Main Points	Notes

Continued on page:

Summary:

Class		Date	
Topic		Continued from Page:	

Main Points	Notes

Continued on page:

Summary:

Made in the USA
Las Vegas, NV
29 December 2024

15573868R00070